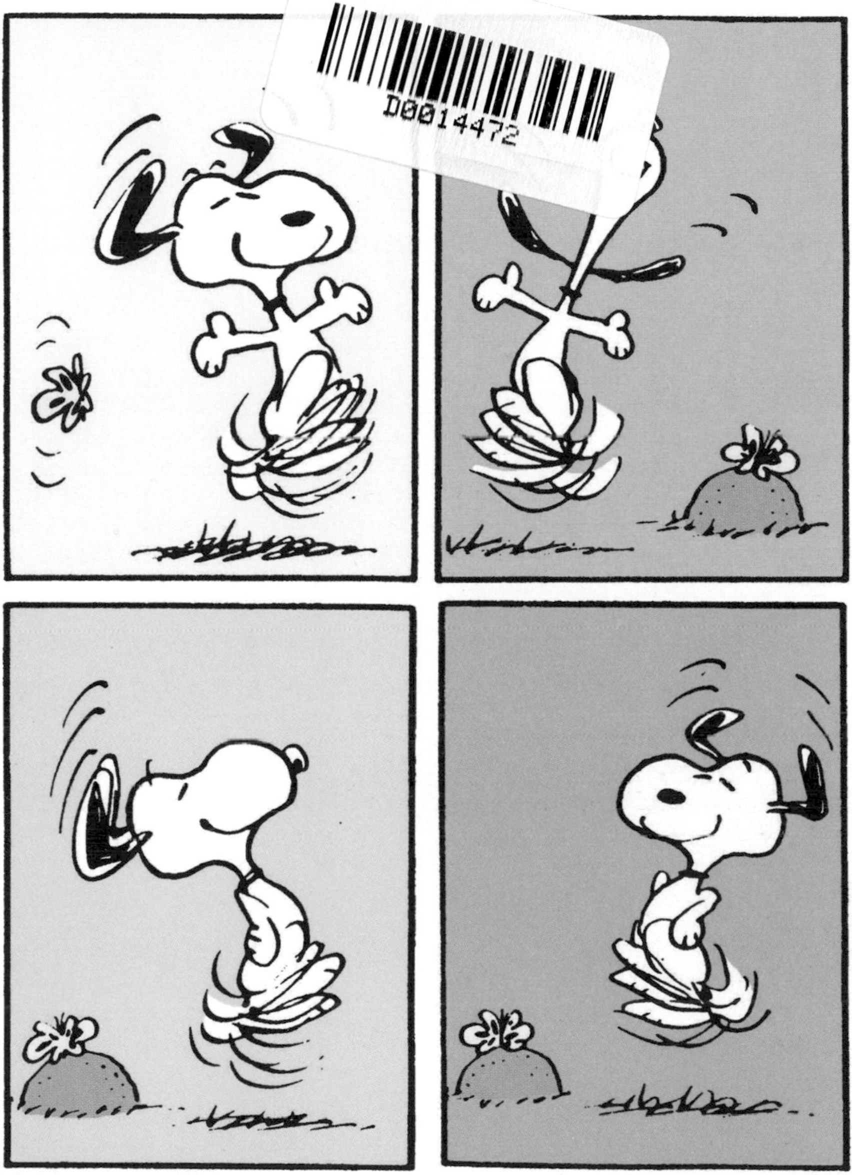

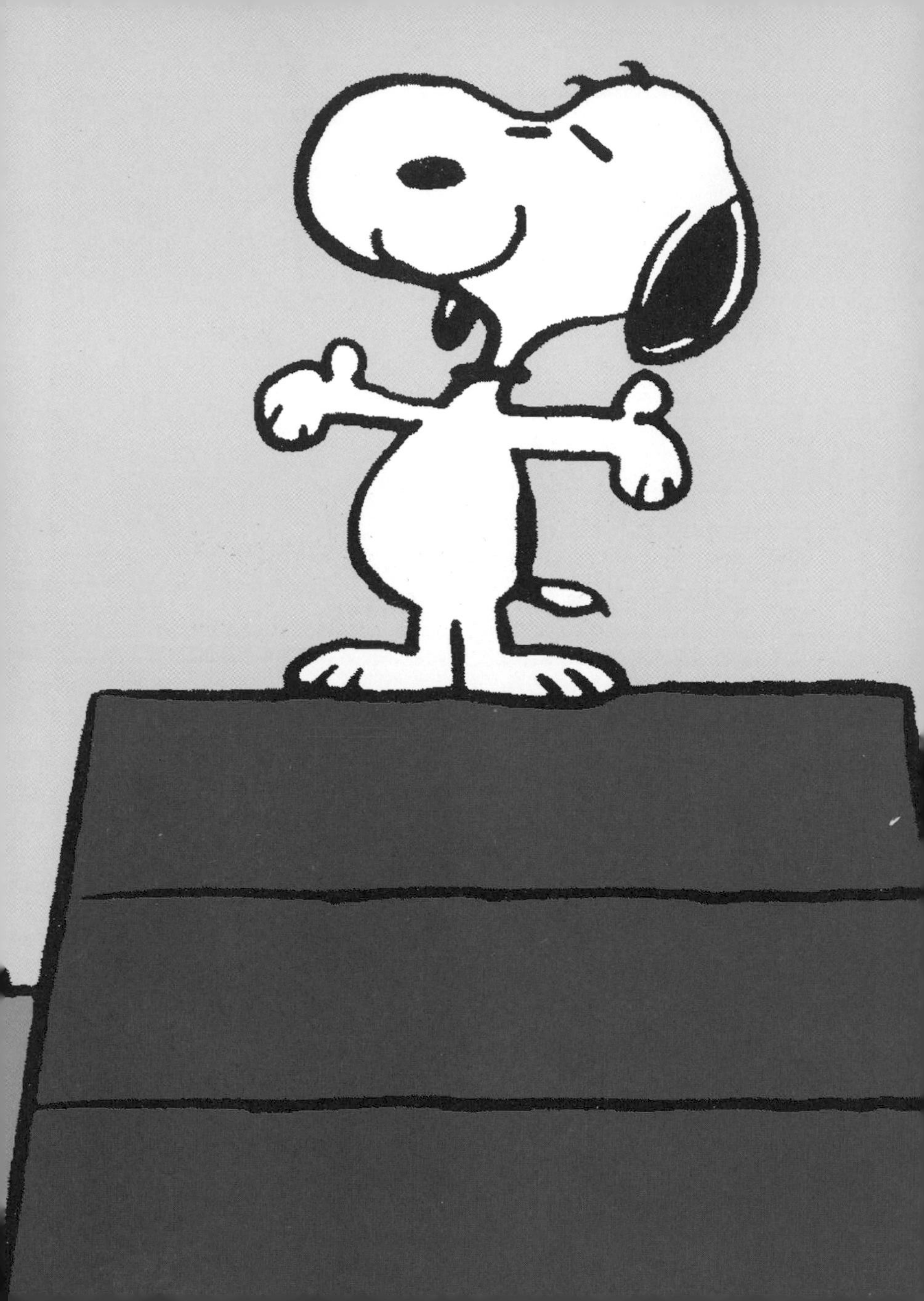

PEANUTS

BE
MORE
SNOOPY

INSPIRED BY THE COMIC STRIP PEANUTS,
CREATED BY CHARLES M. SCHULZ

Written by Nat Gertler

CONTENTS

A DOGGED PURSUIT OF THE GOOD LIFE

Does life feel a little dreary? Are you being pushed around at work or at school? Then maybe it's time to get out of the doghouse and get on top of it all. When you see things from Snoopy's angle, you'll gain a whole new perspective on life. This buoyant beagle can show you the value of imagination and shaking off negativity. In Snoopy's world, you can be anything you want—a Flying Ace, A World Famous Golf Pro, a Masked Marvel, or Head Beagle.

Let *Be More Snoopy* be your guide to bringing more of that beagly joy into your own life. Dance, surf, and live without minding who's watching—and ride out the waves of life with unabashed freedom.

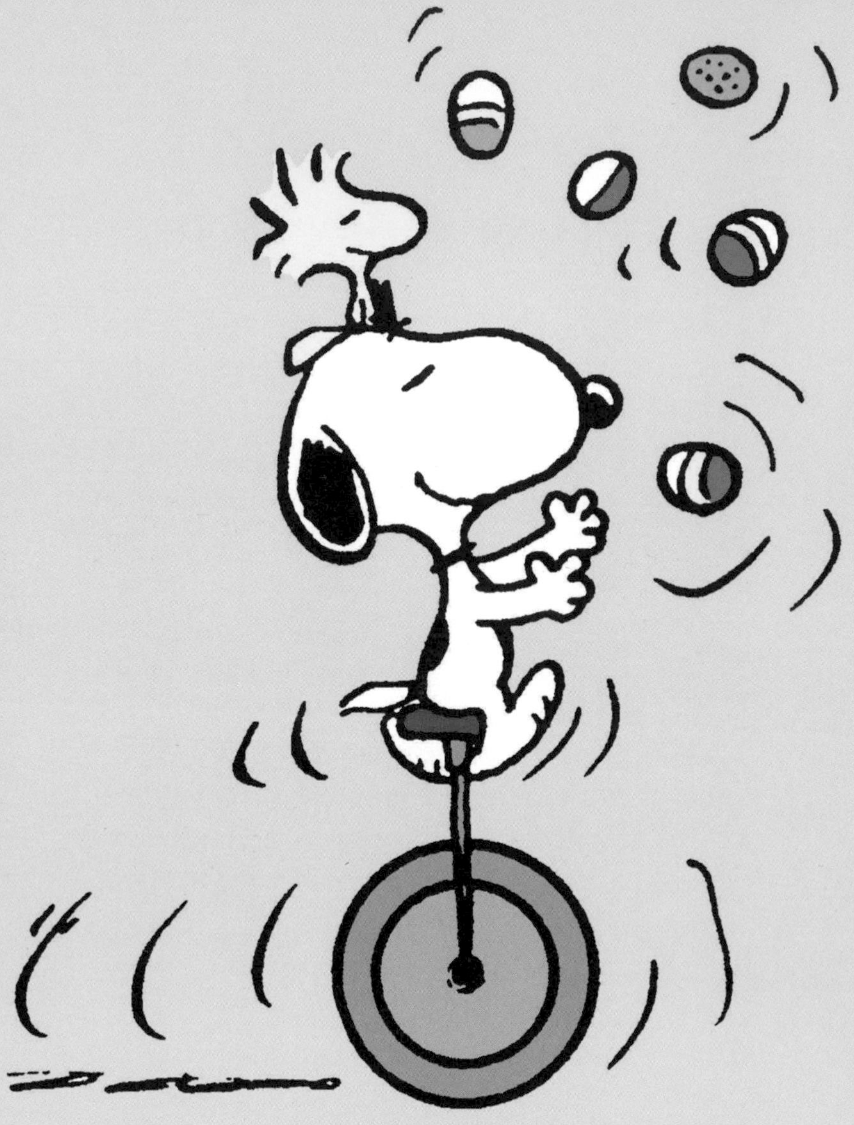

FIND YOUR HAPPY

Joy is a personal experience. Everyone has their own sources. Schroeder finds joy mainly in mastering Beethoven on a toy piano, whereas Snoopy seems to find it anywhere—even juggling on a unicycle. Treasure the sources of joy you do have, but never stop looking for new ones. Look and see: you may find your happy in surprising places.

"YEAHH! IT'S SUPPERTIME!!"
Snoopy

EMBRACE DAILY LIFE

The things that bring you joy don't need to be extraordinary. A snooze in the sunshine, a game of baseball, or a cuddle from a warm puppy can really brighten your day. Never underestimate the simple pleasures, like a stack of warm pancakes. There's a reason Snoopy's favorite three words are "feed the dog"! Regular meals, daydreams, and visits from a good friend—even the feathered kind—can keep many of us happy. If you can recognize the healthy pleasures that already permeate your life, then you've built yourself a firm platform for ongoing joy—as solid and dependable as the roof beneath your head.

"I THINK YOU SHOULD TRY IT
BECAUSE IN MEDICAL TERMS, YOU HAVE
WHAT WE CALL THE 'NEED TO TRY IT.'"
Lucy Van Pelt

TRY NEW THINGS

The world is full of new things to try. Not all of them
will bring you joy, but those that don't will at least
bring you education—as you'll learn to never do them
again! New things don't need to be as challenging as
Linus's ride home on the Snoopy whirlydog. But if you
don't embrace the new, you'll shut yourself off from a
whole world of achievement. Even the act of planning
will give you something to look forward to. So go for
it. Embrace your curiosity—you'll keep wondering
unless you try. Seize the day and step out of
your comfort zone. The doghouse is there
if you need to retreat to safety.

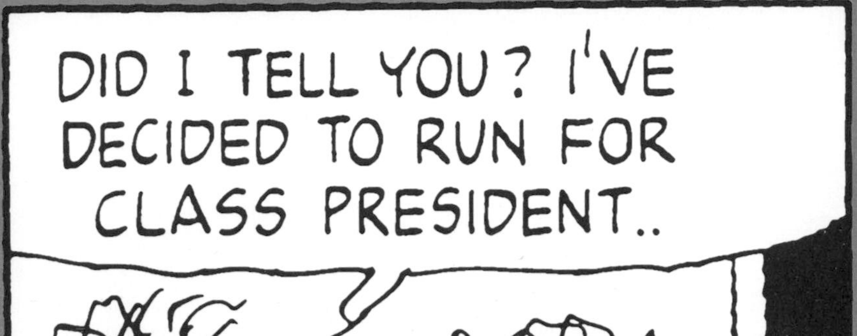
DID I TELL YOU? I'VE DECIDED TO RUN FOR CLASS PRESIDENT..

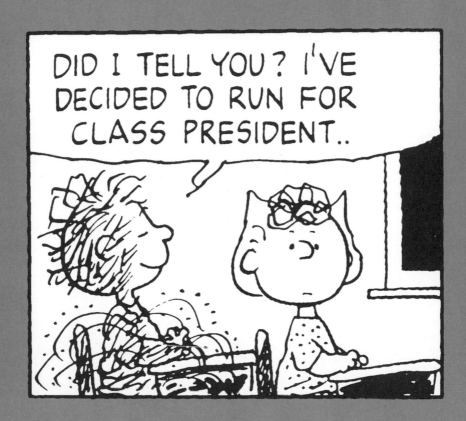

VALUE YOURSELF HIGHLY

Others may see you as filthy, but the dust that covers you may have been trod on by Solomon or Nebuchadnezzar or Genghis Khan. If that thought makes you feel like royalty and worthy of running for class president like it does for Pigpen, hold on to it, and don't let the naysayers convince you that you are anything less. Do not let the cynicism of others taint your view of yourself. Don't change your ways to satisfy others. You are unique as you are, and that is worth celebrating.

"I THINK I'LL JUST LIE HERE
UNTIL THE FIRST SNOW COMES
AND COVERS ME UP ..."
Charlie Brown

ENJOY THE RIDE,
NOT THE DESTINATION

Life is filled with goals that are unmet, but there is
still real joy to be found along the way. Just think of
the happiness to be found in trying to kick a football.
There's the anticipation of the event, the thrill of
running, and then fully investing your effort into a
big, swinging kick. Sure, the ball may be pulled out
of your way, and you may find yourself flying through
the air and landing flat on your back ... but think
of the time you then get to spend laying in the
cool grass and staring at the autumn sky.

"WHEN I THINK OF ALL THOSE
GAMES WE LOST, I GET SICK."
Charlie Brown

COUNT VICTORIES, NOT LOSSES

Everyone makes mistakes. Embrace your successes and forgive yourself for your failures. What does the Flying Ace do when he is shot down by the Red Baron? He gets up, adjusts his helmet, and takes his Sopwith Camel right back into the air. Next time, *he* might be the victor! Every time you step up to the pitcher's mound, you have a fresh chance to play a perfect game, no matter how many times you lost before. And remember—winning a trophy is still a victory, even if it is just for "rookie of the year".

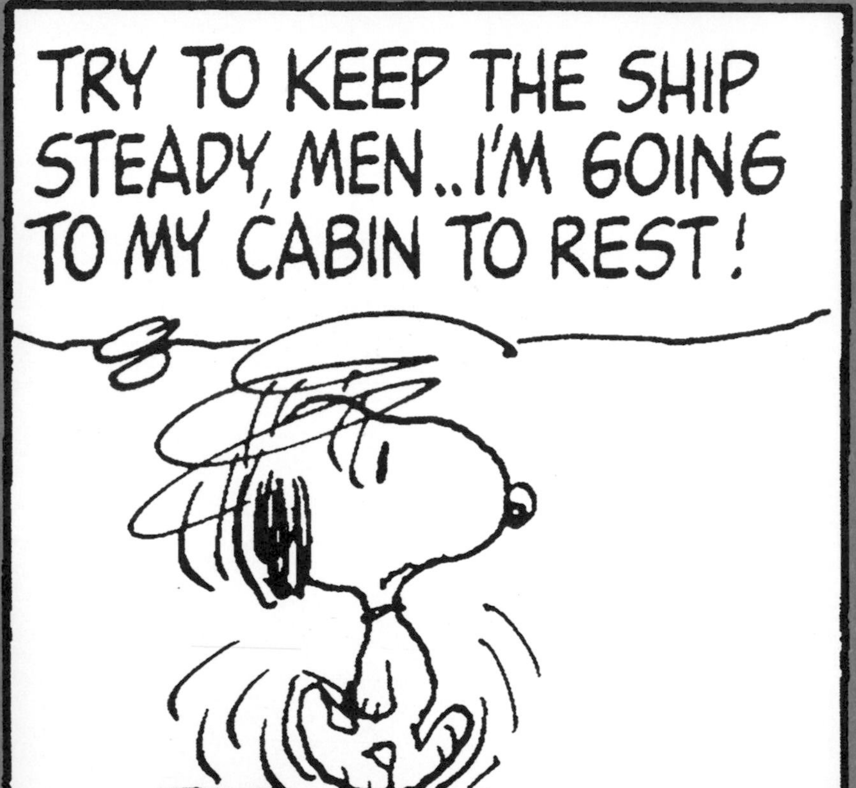
TRY TO KEEP THE SHIP STEADY, MEN..I'M GOING TO MY CABIN TO REST!

PRACTICE
SELF-CARE

Sometimes, everyone wants you to heel when what
you need is to heal. When life throws you a curveball,
be kind to yourself. After all, only you know what you
really need. Only you can hear those chocolate-chip
cookies calling to you from your doghouse. Hold on
tight to your security blanket; take a nap; have five
minutes to yourself. Take your time and come back
when you're ready. The world can't end today—
it's already tomorrow in Australia.

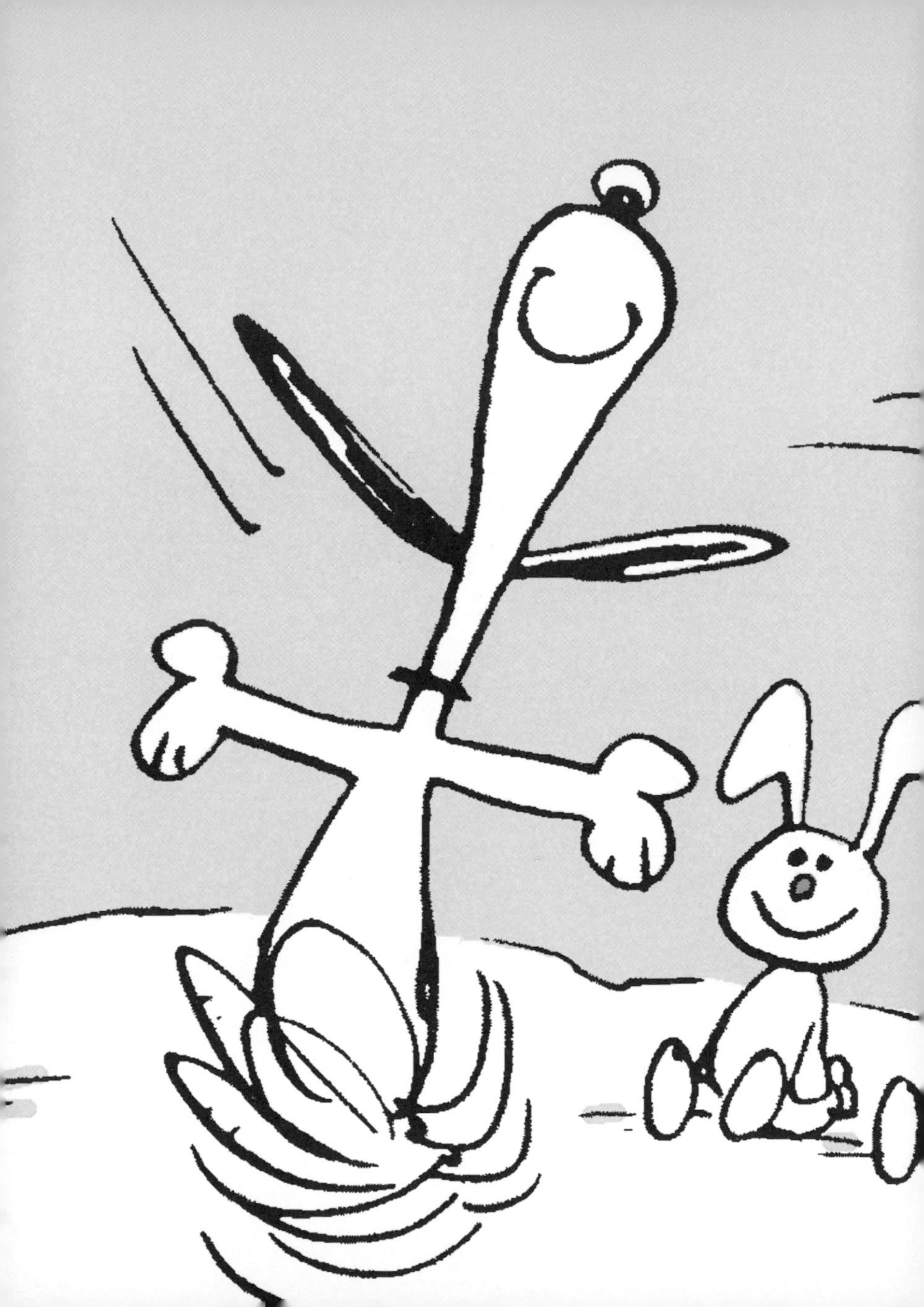

SHOW YOUR JOY

While joy starts from the inside, its glow naturally flows outward, from your heart to your feet, your floppy ears, and your little black nose. Showing your joy keeps it flowing and keeps you going! Keep practicing and soon your grin may shine so brightly that it becomes the only visible part of you.

"ISN'T THAT YOUR DOG
OUT THERE, CHARLIE BROWN?
I THINK HE'S LOST HIS MIND!"
Linus

SHAKE OFF YOUR RESERVATIONS

Your joy is your own to find, feel, and celebrate.
If it's not what others want or expect, that's on them.
They want you to hunt rabbits, but you want to dance
with the bunnies instead? Dance! They want you to
be a "normal dog," but you want to be a Flying Ace?
Fly! Let them erect their "No Dogs Allowed" signs
wherever they wish; it won't stop you from
allowing yourself to be the beagle that you
are—loud, proud, and out of control.

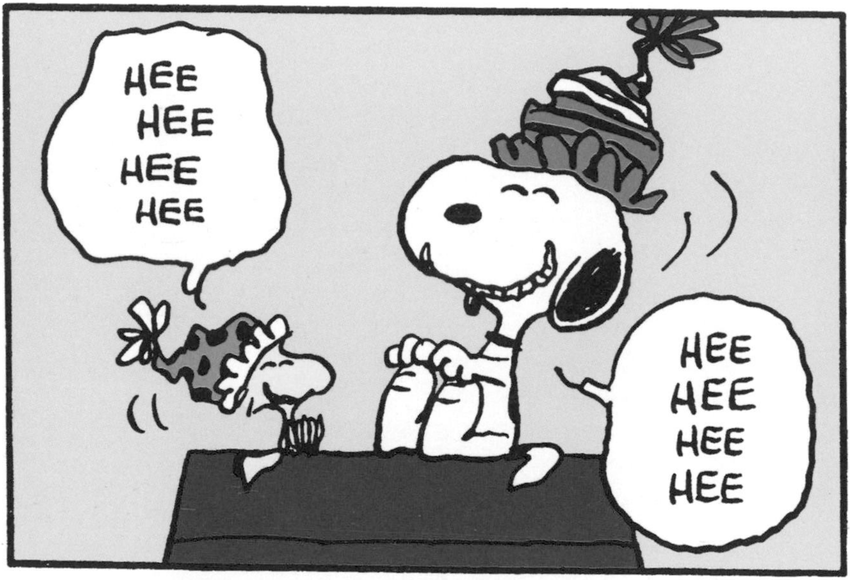
HEE HEE HEE HEE
HEE HEE HEE HEE

SHARE
THE JOKE

Fun is not something to be hoarded. Sharing the
things that delight you can make others joyful, too.
When their joy shines back at you, you'll feel happier
still. So settle down with Snoopy to quaff a root beer,
wish a harmonious happy birthday to Beethoven with
Schroeder, or give in to the giggles with Woodstock.
Laughter is infectious—let it flow in. The rising
tide of joy will then lift everyone's boats.

"PUT A RECORD ON,
SWEETIE ... I'M READY!"
Snoopy

DON'T WAIT
FOR AN EXCUSE

You don't need to wait for a special occasion to
bring out your happy dance. If you did, you might be
waiting forever. Being joyful will make the occasion
special. And if anyone tells you that with all the
trouble in the world you have no right to be happy,
don't believe them. Being upbeat can make troubles
easier to handle. Find pleasure in the small things.
For Snoopy, a sudden snowfall or a passing butterfly
is reason enough to grab a partner and dance!

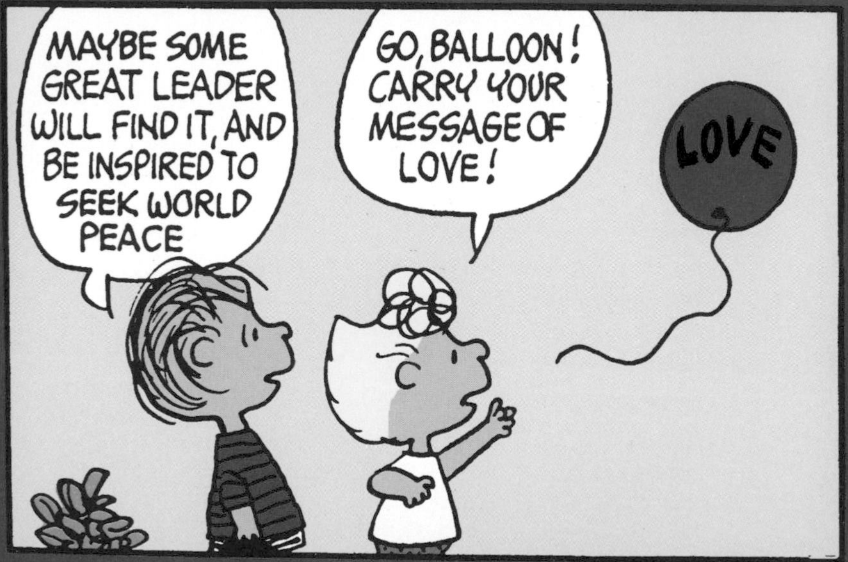
MAYBE SOME GREAT LEADER WILL FIND IT, AND BE INSPIRED TO SEEK WORLD PEACE
GO, BALLOON! CARRY YOUR MESSAGE OF LOVE!
LOVE

SPREAD THE WORD

Think you've found the key to making the world a better place? By sharing the source of your joy, you can become an inspiration to others. While they may never get on board with your life philosophy (or sit down with you and wait for the Great Pumpkin to arrive), they will nevertheless feel the passion in your heart. Maybe, just maybe, that will inspire them to seek out their own source of joy and set them on a path to their own life goal. By spreading the word, you let others know that joy is possible.

STOMP! STOMP! STOMP! STOMP!

"JUST THINKING ABOUT IT MAKES ME SO MAD ..."
Snoopy

ACKNOWLEDGE YOUR ANGER

Life is not full of endless sunshine and home runs. Sometimes, you have to release your anger, because your anger will not release you. While anger can be useful if it drives you to address a problem, it can become destructive if unchecked. So stomp on that tennis racket; kick that water dish; or release a good, long, loud "AAUGH!" As long as you do not hurt yourself or someone else, giving your anger a physical or audible manifestation may allow you to move on. Then you can step back onto the tennis court, send your manuscript to another publisher, or face whatever opportunities life brings next.

"ANYONE WHO RETURNS
FROM A LONG TRIP SHOULD BE
GREETED WITH A BEAGLE HUG!"
Snoopy

MAKE YOUR BUSINESS JOYFUL

When you think of business, you think of cold, hard cash rather than all things warm and joyous. But you don't have to be torn between the need to make money and the desire to feel joy—instead, combine the two! You might not have much luck selling warm hugs (that usually only works if you're a puppy), but you could try selling warm cookies. If you're really lucky, you might be able to trade your music, dance, or storytelling skills for a little financial joy. And your enterprise might make others happy in the process.

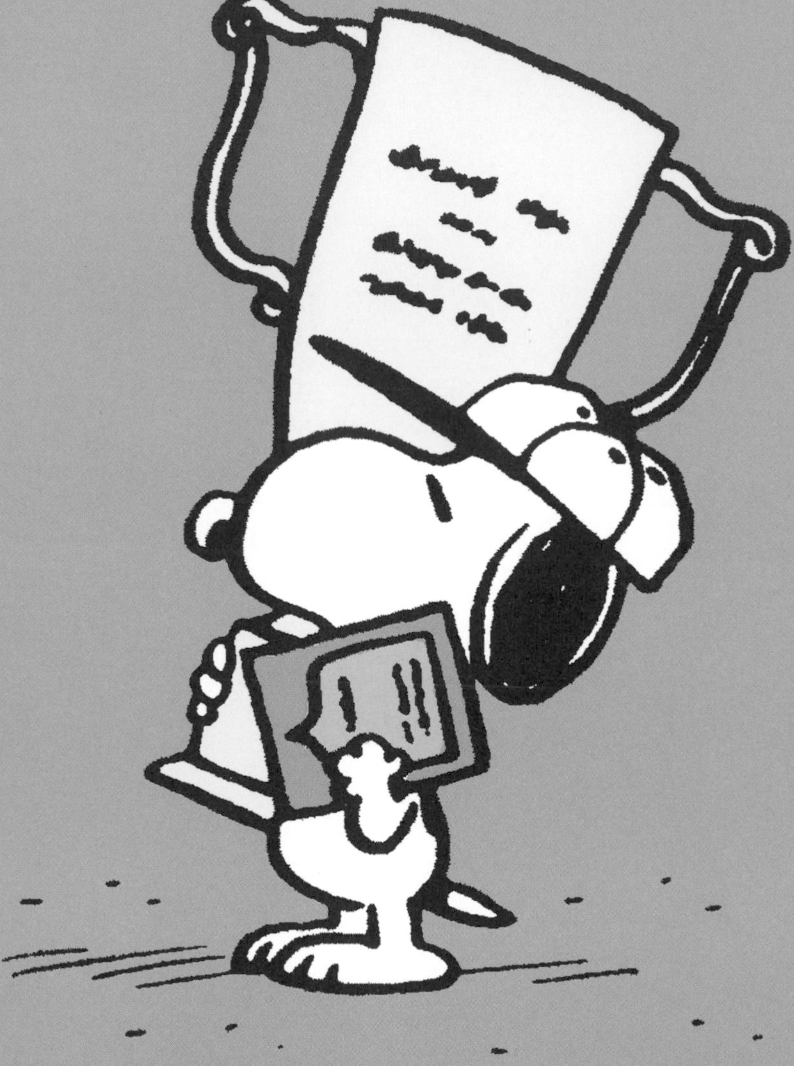

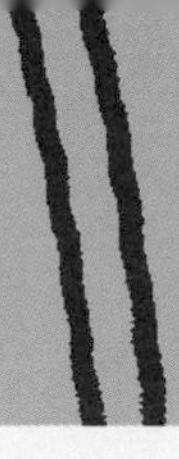

BE WORLD FAMOUS

Being a jack-of-all-trades may get you by, but why settle for being a jack when you could be a king? When you could, in fact, be World Famous? Whatever dreams you're pursuing, whatever skills you're learning, make excellence your goal. Like Snoopy, reach for the sky—with both paws.

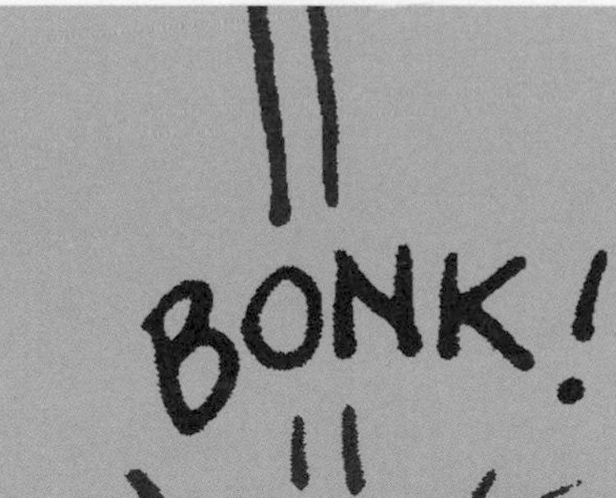
BONK!

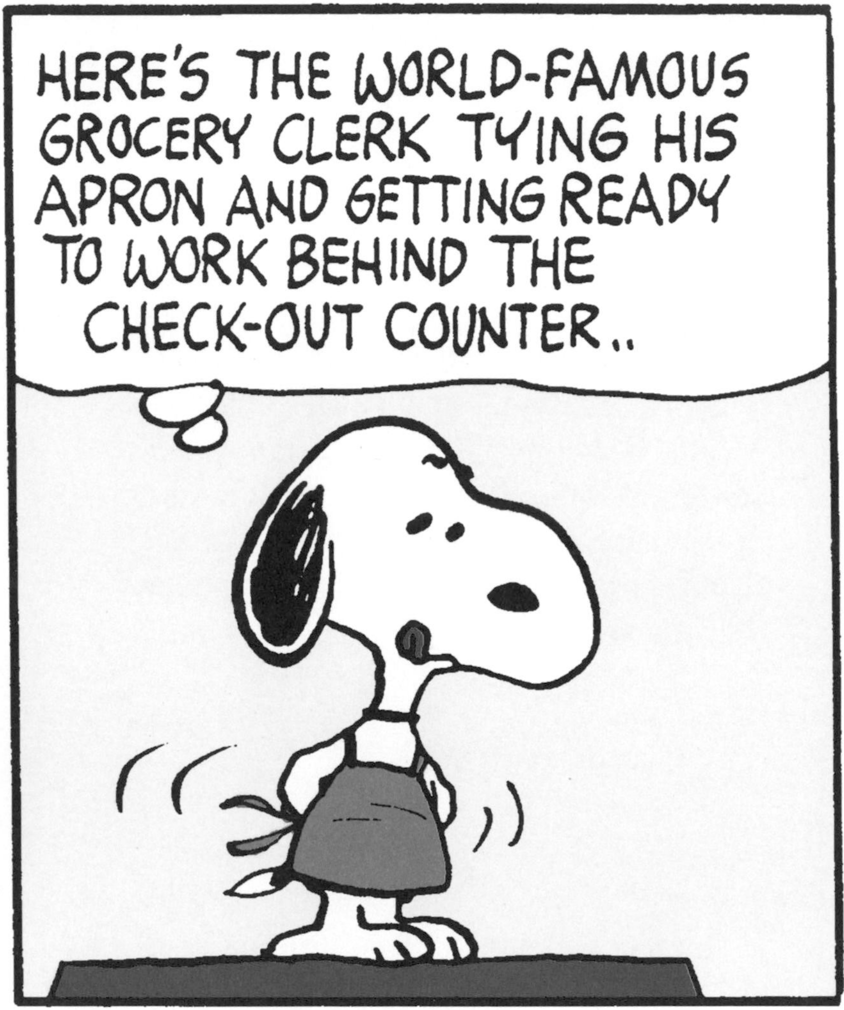
HERE'S THE WORLD-FAMOUS GROCERY CLERK TYING HIS APRON AND GETTING READY TO WORK BEHIND THE CHECK-OUT COUNTER..

AIM FOR EXCELLENCE

Whatever you do, be like Snoopy and act as if
the whole world is watching. Being World Famous
is all about attitude. It doesn't matter if the fame is
only in your own mind. Role-playing bagging up bread,
beans, and jelly? Counting out the change for six
bags of carrots? Even working behind an imaginary
check-out counter gives you the opportunity to shine.
Take your reputation into your own paws and
be the very best you can be.

"HE PUTS ON A VERY
GOOD SHOW, DOESN'T HE?
I'M VERY IMPRESSED ..."
Charlie Brown

MAKE A SHOW OF IT

People pay more attention when you throw
in a little flair. Putting on a pawpet show?
Use all the paws you can. Selling wreaths door
to door? If carrying one wreath on your nose sells
one, try twirling two more at the same time so you
sell three! Juggle the Easter eggs; dance with a
(candy) cane and top hat. Make every moment an
event, and every event a grand occasion—
with you in the starring role!

"I'M INTERESTED ONLY IN WHAT
PEOPLE THINK OF ME AS I **ENTER**
THE ROOM. I DON'T CARE WHAT
THEY THINK OF ME AS I **LEAVE!**"
Linus

FIRST
IMPRESSIONS COUNT

If you want people to think well of you, it's worth
putting in a bit of effort. After all, you only get to
meet someone for the first time once. Tip your top
hat when you say hello. Shine your shoes. Treat every
new person you meet like they're an old friend who
might have candy in their pocket. No matter whether
you have two feet or four, start off on the right one.
Make sure they'll remember you—and that
the memory will be a good one!

"BUT IT'S JUST NOT
THE SORT OF THING YOU
WEAR EVERY DAY!"
Snoopy

DRESS THE PART

If you want to play the part, dress the part!
Snoopy has an outfit for a variety of characters—
the detective has his deerstalker, the lawyer his
bowler, and the foreign legionnaire his kepi. Why not
do the same? Throw on the threads of a smart,
confident character and watch the change in how
people react to you. You'll probably find yourself
thinking in a whole new way. Until tomorrow,
of course, when it will be time to hang up your
flying helmet and pick another persona!

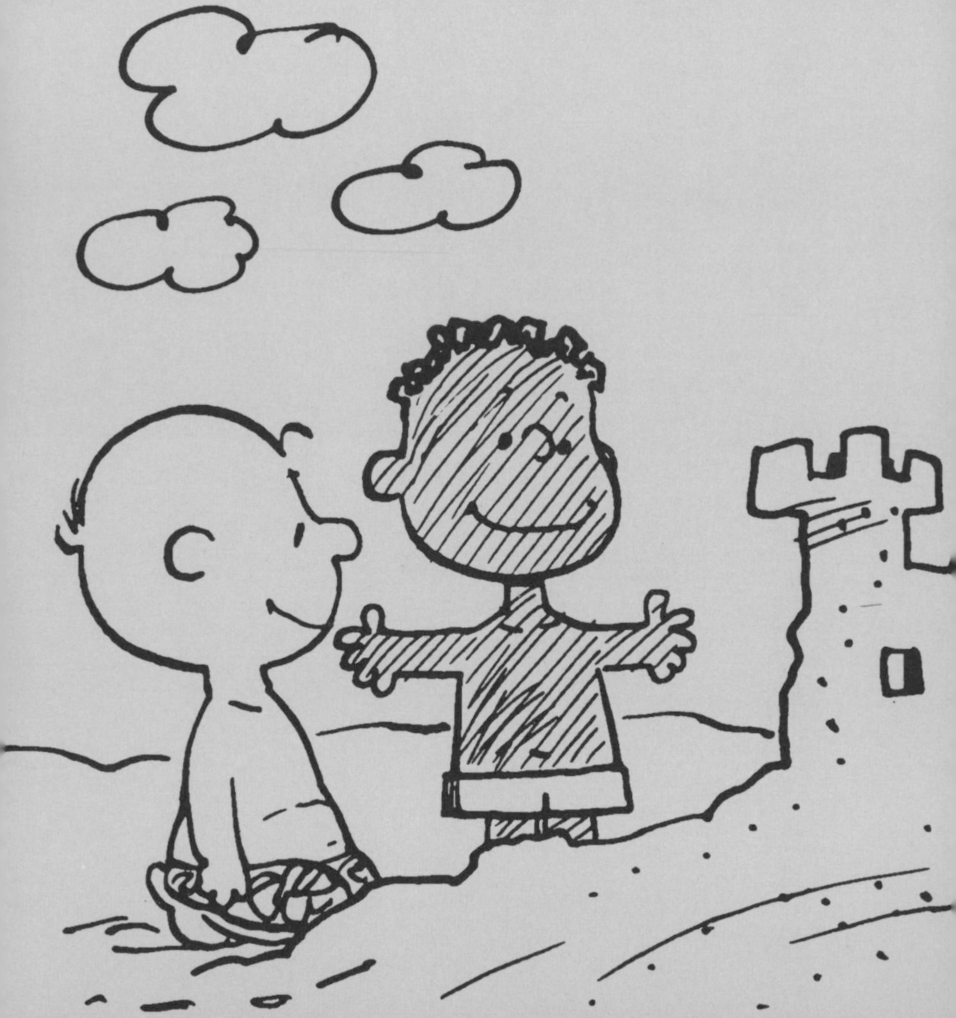

BE A FRIEND OF FRIENDS

We all need friends, whether they are furry, feathered, or human. Friends accept you for who you are. They won't try to change you (even if they keep calling you "sir," like Marcie does). That's true whether it's a group of pals or an extra-special buddy who goes everywhere with you. Sandcastles on the beach may wash away, but friendships are built of stronger, more lasting stuff.

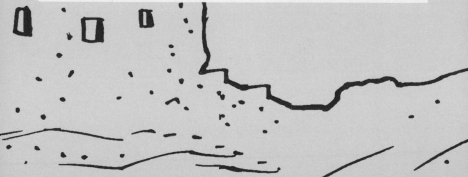

"**REAL** PENGUINS DON'T
GET COLD FEET!"
Charlie Brown

WALK A MILE IN SOMEONE ELSE'S FEET

In friendship, empathy is everything. You can't give your friend the support they need unless you can imagine living through what they are living through. You may not fully understand why it's such a big deal when your buddy's sister turns his blanket into a kite and lets it sail away, but no matter. He's hurting, so you're right there with him hurting, too. Employ your skills for imagination: sit with them and share their pain, because next time it might be your turn.

"YOU'RE WEIRD, SIR, BUT
YOU'RE A LOT OF FUN."
Marcie

IDENTIFY
YOUR FRIENDS

Friends don't always show their feelings for you
with hugs and kisses! There are a thousand ways
people (or dogs, or birds) can show their friendship
every day, so you have to pay attention. Maybe they
make sure your water bowl is always topped up.
Maybe they sit and listen while you babble away
for hours. Maybe they let you pitch even when
the team only wins when you're not there.
Know who your friends are, and remember
to let them know you know it.

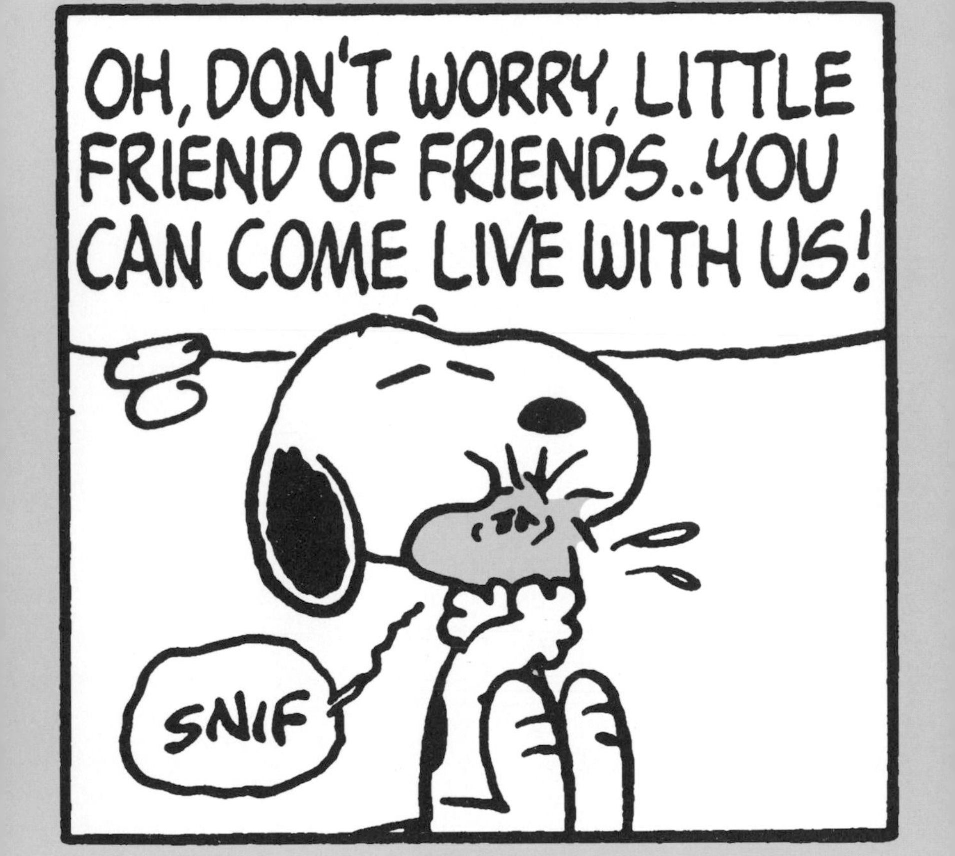
OH, DON'T WORRY, LITTLE FRIEND OF FRIENDS..YOU CAN COME LIVE WITH US!
SNIF

DEMONSTRATE YOU CARE

Never stop looking for ways to brighten your friends'
lives. Be generous with your time and your talents.
You could do something creative, like drawing them
a picture of their favorite composer, or something
practical, like letting them move in with you when
they're in need. While friendships can't be bought,
they do thrive on genuine no-strings-attached
tokens of goodwill. When you feel real friendship,
you'll find a thousand ways to demonstrate it.

"THAT WAS THE BEST VALENTINE'S
DAY EVER, PIGPEN!"

Peppermint Patty

LOVE FREELY

Love is not a limited resource. Love needs no excuse. Love your sweet babboo, even if he doesn't love you back. You can't summon the courage to talk to your favorite little red-haired girl? Love from afar. Love your mother even if she flew away before you were hatched. Send Valentine's Day cards without expecting one back. Adopt Linus's attitude: "I love without reservation! I love without qualification! I love without even thinking!" Just love.

"WELL, A GOOD ATTORNEY
CAN'T SIT BY, AND WATCH
HIS CLIENT TAKE A BEATING."
Snoopy

STAND UP
FOR OTHERS

If a friend is in genuine danger, there's nothing for
it—you may have to put yourself on the line for them.
Maybe your little bird friend is in the vicious claws of
the cat next door. Perhaps your brother is surrounded
by coyotes. Or a local marbles hustler might have
scammed a pal out of their entire sack of marbles.
When the moment comes, take courage. Do not shirk.
Do not run away. Leap heroically into the fray!
Win or lose, you'll be able to hold your head
up high (even if it is a little bruised).

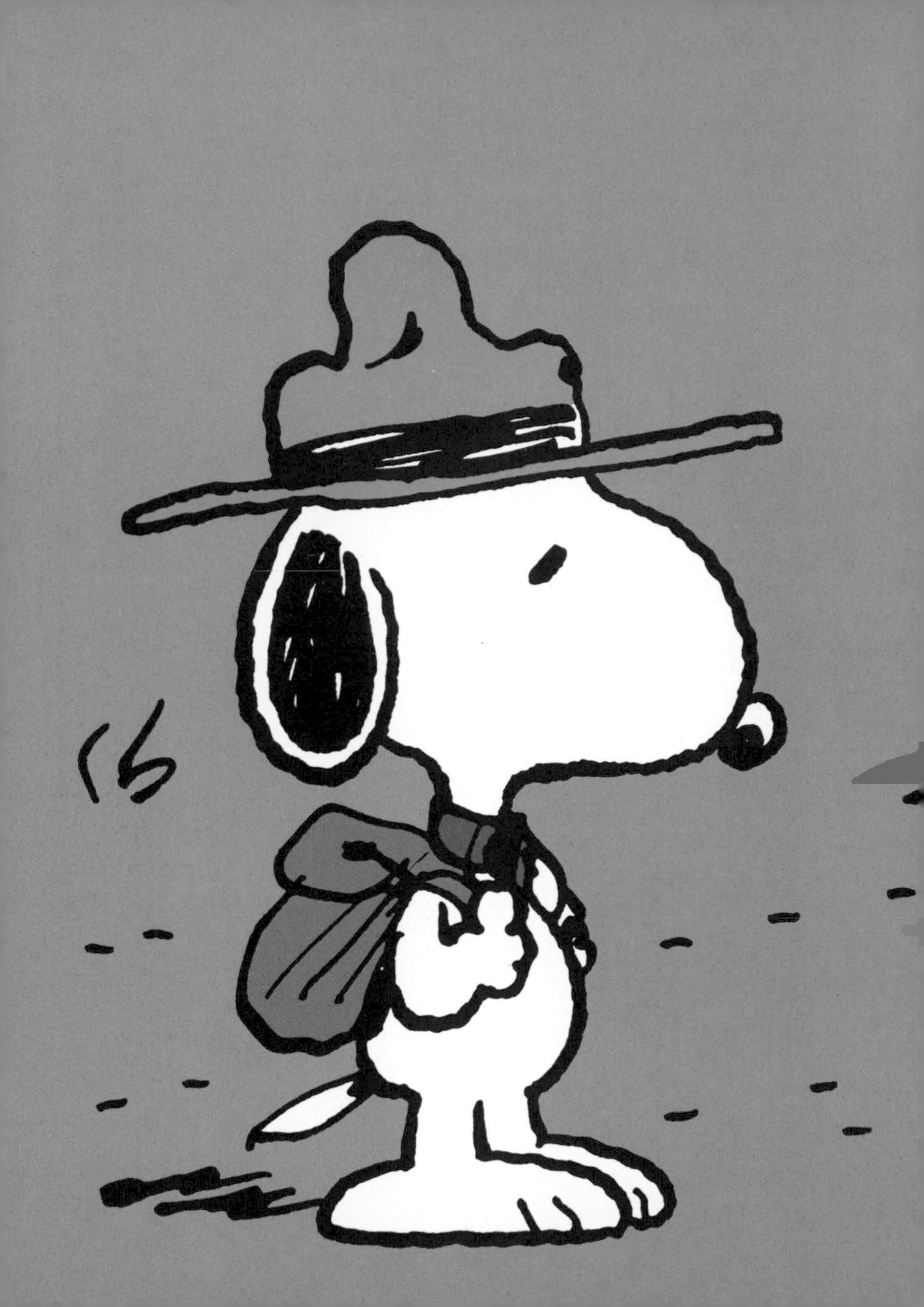

BE HEAD BEAGLE

**Baseball teams need managers.
Beagle Scout troops need troop leaders.
Life offers all sorts of situations where
someone has to take control. Who is
better able than you to do it? Oh, really?
Well, if they're not available, then
it might as well be you!**

"YOU'RE RIGHT ... YOU **WOULD** MAKE A GOOD QUEEN!"
Linus

CHOOSE TO
TAKE CONTROL

According to Lucy, "for every 11 followers born
into this world, there is one leader." Be like Lucy.
Be that one-in-a-dozen leader and take control.
Once you choose a path of power, there are no
limits to what you can do. Don't settle for being
First Lady when you could be President yourself—
or even queen! Just remember not to let power
go to your head. Use it not for your own
good, but for the good you can do.

"NO PROBLEM IS SO BIG OR
SO COMPLICATED THAT IT CAN'T
BE RUN AWAY FROM!"
Linus

AVOID UNNEEDED CONFLICT

Don't seek trouble for its own sake, and don't let trouble seek you. What did Charlie Brown do when the big boys came after him? He organized a discussion group! What did Joe Cool do when one of the guys at the gym wanted to pound him? He assumed the bully wouldn't hit a guy with glasses, and to be safe, he put on seven pairs. A little fast thinking or even faster footwork will get you out of many needless confrontations.

"NOW, AS IN OTHER OF LIFE'S ENDEAVORS, COOPERATION IS VERY IMPORTANT."

Snoopy

SHARE YOUR KNOWLEDGE

As a leader, it's your job to teach those who follow you. Knowledge will make them better followers and, when their time comes, better leaders. Pass on the skills you have, such as how to play pétanque, and share ideas of your own, like Head Beagle Snoopy's theory that clouds cause the wind. Teach the little birdies to fly, or to sail—and don't mind if they're better at it than you are! When you give the gift of knowledge, you give the gift of freedom.

"YOU ALL FORGOT YOUR
BEAGLE SCOUT OATH, 'DON'T
CUT OUT ON A FRIEND.'"
Snoopy

LEAD WHERE OTHERS WILL FOLLOW

A wise leader uses persuasion, not force, to keep their followers following them. Make them feel like they want to go where you want them to go, and you'll never have to worry about them skipping out (even at the siren call of a pepperoni pizza). When you're placed in charge of a team, lead from the front, encourage your troops, don't ask them to do anything you wouldn't do, and remember—a little bit of carrot (or maybe angel food cake with seven-minute frosting) can achieve more than a whole lot of stick.

Senior Editor Emma Grange
Project Art Editor Chris Gould
Editor Julia March
Production Editor Siu Yin Chan
Senior Production Controller Louise Daly
Managing Editor Sarah Harland
Managing Art Editor Vicky Short
Publisher Julie Ferris
Art Director Lisa Lanzarini
Publishing Director Mark Searle

DK would like to thank Nat Gertler for his text,
Craig Herman at Peanuts Worldwide, Alexis Fajardo
and Alena Carnes of Charles M. Schulz Creative Associates,
and Kayla Dugger for editorial assistance.

First American Edition, 2020
Published in the United States by DK Publishing
1450 Broadway, Suite 801, New York, NY 10018

Page design copyright © 2020 Dorling Kindersley Limited
DK, a Division of Penguin Random House LLC
20 21 22 23 24 10 9 8 7 6 5 4 3 2 1
001–321690–Sept/2020

© PEANUTS Worldwide LLC

A catalog record for this book is available
from the Library of Congress.
ISBN: 978-0-7440-2757-0

DK books are available at special discounts when purchased in bulk
for sales promotions, premiums, fund-raising, or educational use.
For details, contact: DK Publishing Special Markets,
1450 Broadway, Suite 801, New York, NY 10018
SpecialSales@dk.com

Printed and bound in China

For the curious

www.dk.com

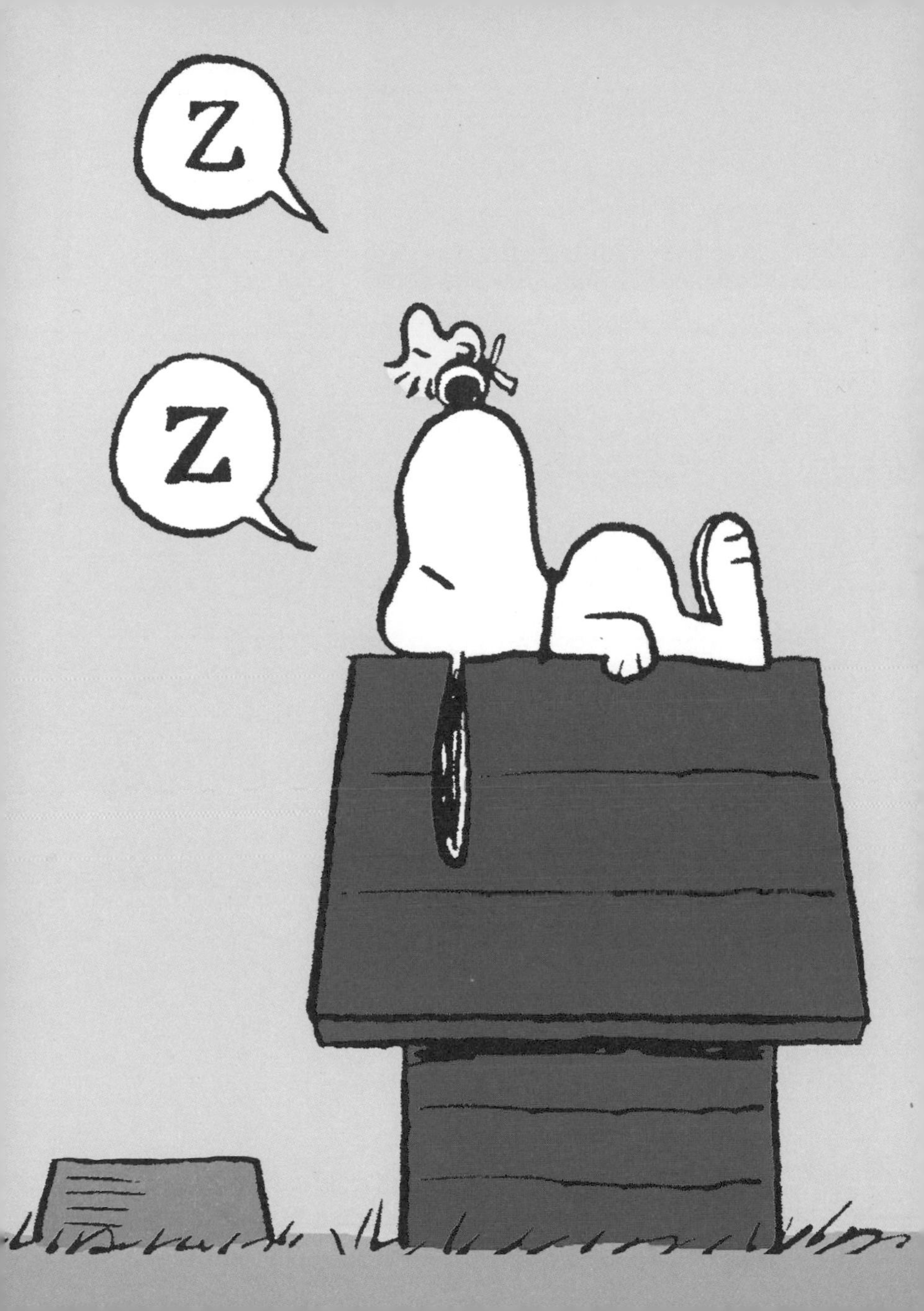
Z
Z

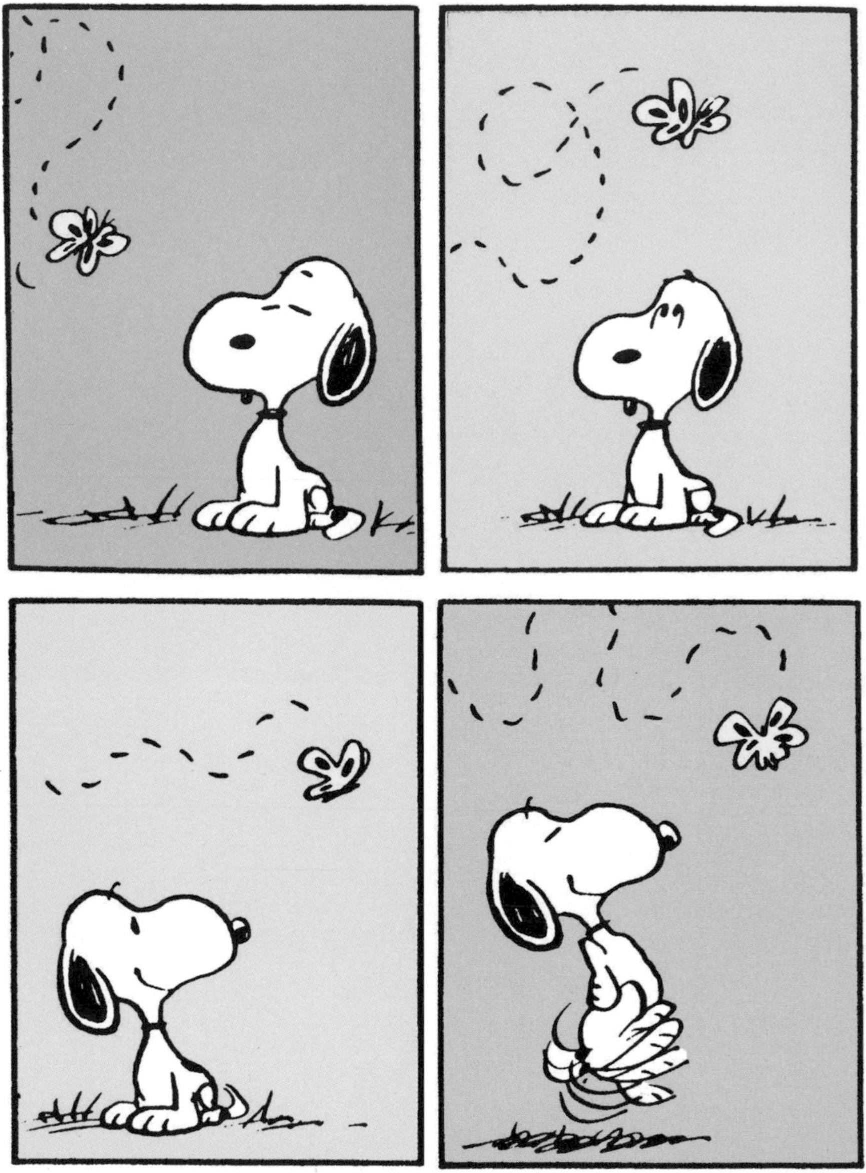